TULSA CITY-COUNTY LIBRARY

D0912915

MRJC
2/10

SAYINGS and PHRASES

It's as Clear as a Bell!

(And Other Curious Things We Say)

written by Cynthia Klingel ★ illustrated by Mernie Gallagher-Cole

ABOUT THE AUTHOR

As a high school English teacher and as an elementary teacher, Cynthia Klingel has shared her love of language with students. She has always been fascinated with idioms and figures of speech. Today Cynthia is a school district administrator in Minnesota. She has two daughters who also share her love of language through reading, writing, and talking!

ABOUT THE ILLUSTRATOR

Mernie Gallagher-Cole lives in Pennsylvania with her husband and two children. She uses sayings and phrases like the ones in this book every day. She has illustrated many children's books, including *Messy Molly* and *Día De Los Muertos* for The Child's World®.

The Child's World®

Published in the United States of America by The Child's World®
1980 Lookout Drive • Mankato, MN 56003-1705
800-599-READ • www.childsworld.com

ACKNOWLEDGMENTS
The Child's World®: Mary Berendes, Publishing Director

Katherine Stevenson: Editing

The Design Lab: Kathleen Petelinsek, Design;
Victoria Stanley, Page Production

Copyright © 2010 by The Child's World®
All rights reserved. No part of this book may be reproduced or utilized in any form or by any means without written permission from the publisher.

LIBRARY OF CONGRESS CATALOGING-IN-PUBLICATION DATA
Klingel, Cynthia Fitterer.
  It's as clear as a bell! (and other curious things we say) / by Cynthia Klingel.
    p. cm. — (Sayings and phrases)
  ISBN 978-1-60253-208-3 (library bound : alk. paper)
  1. English language—Idioms—Juvenile literature.
  2. Figures of speech—Juvenile literature. I. Title. II. Series.
  PE1460.K6845 2009
  428.1—dc22   2009001641

People use idioms
(ID-ee-umz) every day.
These are sayings and
phrases with meanings that
are different from the actual
words. Some idioms seem silly.
Many of them don't make
much sense . . . at first.

This book will help you
understand some of the most
common idioms. It will tell
you how you might hear a
saying or phrase. It will tell
you what the saying really
means. All of these sayings
and short phrases—even the
silly ones—are an important
part of our language!

TABLE of CONTENTS

All that glitters is not gold

Nine-year-old Madison was excited. "Todd just got a job at a movie theater," she said. "I'd like to work there, too. I love watching movies!"

"Do you know what Todd does?" asked Mom.

"Not exactly," said Madison.

"He sells tickets and then cleans up after the show," she replied. "He doesn't get to watch the movies. Working in a theater might seem like your dream job. But remember—all that glitters is not gold!"

MEANING: Things aren't always as nice as they seem

As happy as a clam

Aunt Emily left two-year-old Nathan at Jon's house for the afternoon. Nathan was cranky at first and didn't want to play. Jon finally gave up and went outside. When he came back in, he asked his mom if Nathan was in a better mood.

"He sure is," said Jon's mom. "I let him play with some of your old cars. He loves them! Look at him—he's as happy as a clam."

MEANING: Enjoying what you are doing; in a good mood; happy and content

Beauty is in the eye of the beholder

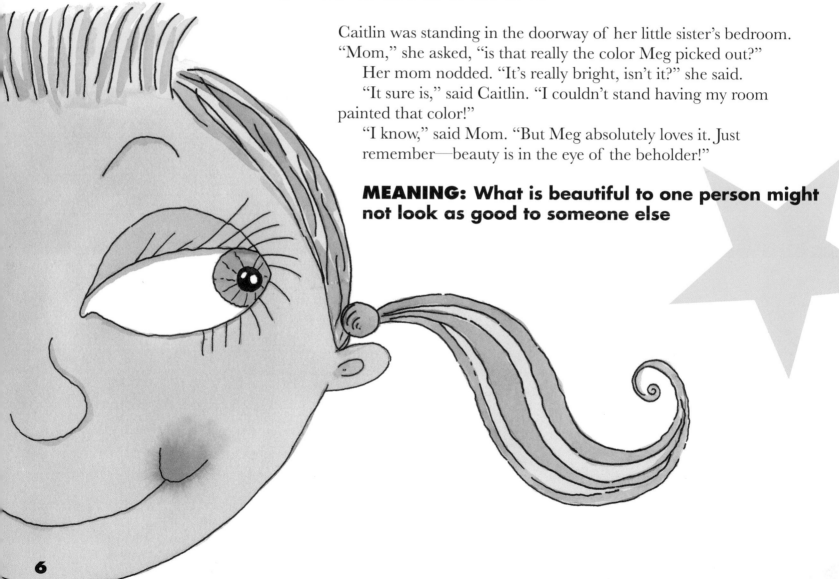

Caitlin was standing in the doorway of her little sister's bedroom. "Mom," she asked, "is that really the color Meg picked out?"

Her mom nodded. "It's really bright, isn't it?" she said.

"It sure is," said Caitlin. "I couldn't stand having my room painted that color!"

"I know," said Mom. "But Meg absolutely loves it. Just remember—beauty is in the eye of the beholder!"

MEANING: What is beautiful to one person might not look as good to someone else

6

Bite your tongue

Anna had just come from softball practice.

"How did it go?" asked her dad.

"It was really frustrating," said Anna. "Molly kept complaining again. She only joined the team a month ago, but she thinks she knows everything! Mom said just to ignore her, but it's hard. When Molly started complaining about Kayla's pitching, I really had to bite my tongue!"

MEANING: To keep yourself from saying something you might regret

A bull in a china shop

Noah's family had a gigantic dog named Ace. Noah was really excited—Ace had just passed his test to be a therapy dog! Now he would be able to visit people who were sick or feeling sad.

"Where are we going to take him?" Noah asked his mom. "Can he go to that nursing home where Grandma Doyle used to live? They'd love him there!"

"They sure would," agreed Mom. "But he's kind of big and clumsy for a place like that. He'd be like a bull in a china shop!"

MEANING: Something that is out of place, or clumsy in a situation that calls for great care

Can't see the forest for the trees

"How does Aunt Sophie like her new job?" asked Ryan.

"She's not sure yet," Ryan's mom replied. "She's feeling a little frustrated because there's so much to learn."

"Right now, Aunt Sophie can't see the forest for the trees," explained Dad. "She's so busy trying to learn all the little parts of her job that she can't even think about what it all means."

MEANING: To pay so much attention to details that you don't see the big picture; to focus on small details and not understand the whole situation

A chicken with its head cut off

Sarah had been helping her mom all morning, getting ready for Grandma's big birthday party.

"How are we doing, Mom?" Sarah asked.

"Well," answered Mom, "everyone will be here in an hour, and there's still a lot to do! I need a minute to think about what to do next. Otherwise I'll just be running around like a chicken with its head cut off!"

MEANING: Disorganized; doing things but not finishing anything

Clear as a bell

Simon and his brother were having a water fight when their dad came outside to find them.

"OK, guys," said Dad to the two boys, "you need to put the hose down for a while. I'd like to get those roses planted before your mom gets home. She'll really be happy! But we're going to have to work fast. No more playing around until we're done! Is that clear?"

"Clear as a bell!" said Simon. He grinned at his brother. "We can settle this later."

MEANING: Clearly understood

Cute as a bug's ear

Aunt Emily heard voices through her front door. "Trick or treat!" the voices said.

When Aunt Emily opened the door, Jake and his whole family cried, "Happy Halloween!" All of the kids were wearing costumes.

"Oh my!" said Aunt Emily with a smile. "I see a ghost, and a witch, and… well, will you look at that? It's little Amy, dressed up as a pumpkin! She's as cute as a bug's ear!"

MEANING: Very cute

Double whammy

Uncle Peter called his nephew Eric on the phone. "Hey, buddy," he said when Eric answered. "Your dad told me about your skateboard accident. How are you feeling?"

"Terrible," said Peter. "First I break my ankle, and then I catch this stupid cold. All I can do is sit on the couch. I'm really bored!"

"A broken ankle and a cold? You poor guy, that's really a double whammy! Why don't I bring over a movie and keep you company for a while?"

MEANING: Two bad things happening at the same time

Ducks in a row

Corey's big sister Kristin had been in her room all day, with the door shut. "What's she up to?" Corey asked their mom. "That seems really weird."

"Well, remember," said Mom, "she's got that college interview on Friday. She really wants to make a good impression, so she's spending a lot of time getting everything ready. She needs to have all her ducks in a row."

MEANING: To have everything in order

Fresh as a daisy

Kelly came back from the park early.

"Did you have fun?" Kelly's mom asked.

"Not me," Kelly replied. "It's too hot out! But Dawn had a great time."

"Dawn is just like her mother," said Kelly's mom with a laugh. "The heat doesn't bother her, and she never seems tired. Everyone else can be exhausted and dripping wet, but she's always fresh as a daisy!"

MEANING: Well rested; full of energy

The handwriting is on the wall

Zach and his friends were worried. The city was thinking about redoing Century Park and replacing the skate park with tennis courts. Zach's dad had just talked to a friend on the city council.

"Well," said Dad, "the good news is that they're going to expand the other skate park down by the river. But where Century Park is concerned, I'm afraid the handwriting is on the wall. They're going to tear down that skate park next week."

MEANING: A warning sign that something bad is going to happen

Jack of all trades

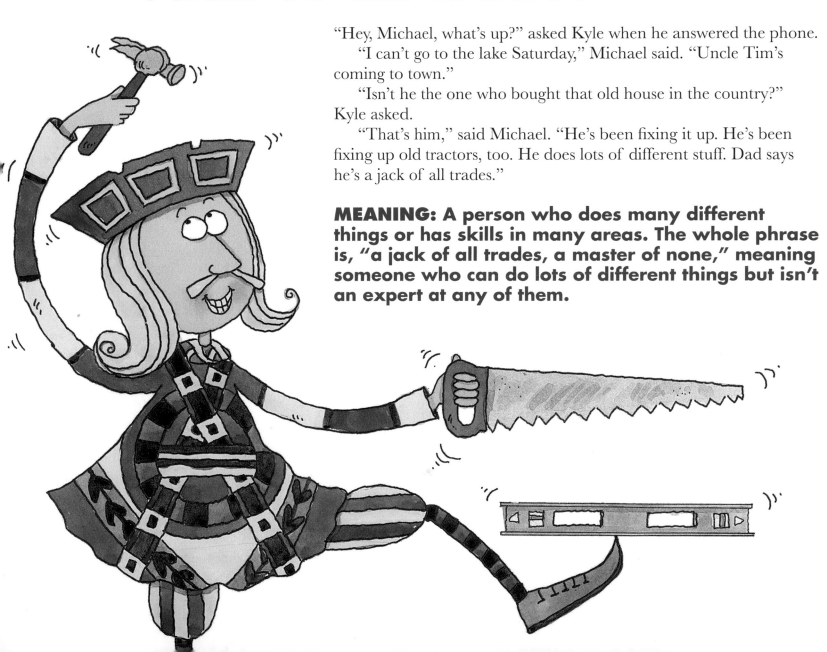

"Hey, Michael, what's up?" asked Kyle when he answered the phone.

"I can't go to the lake Saturday," Michael said. "Uncle Tim's coming to town."

"Isn't he the one who bought that old house in the country?" Kyle asked.

"That's him," said Michael. "He's been fixing it up. He's been fixing up old tractors, too. He does lots of different stuff. Dad says he's a jack of all trades."

MEANING: A person who does many different things or has skills in many areas. The whole phrase is, "a jack of all trades, a master of none," meaning someone who can do lots of different things but isn't an expert at any of them.

Kick up your heels

Charlie's mom had been working overtime on a big project. Finally, she was done.

"Congratulations!" said Charlie's dad. "What are you going to do to celebrate?"

"Well," said Mom, "Roberta asked if I wanted to drive into the city to go shopping tomorrow, but I have a lot of catching up to do."

"Oh, go ahead!" said Dad. "You've been working really hard. Why don't you kick up your heels and have a little fun!"

MEANING: To celebrate; to have fun

Knee-jerk reaction

Patrick's dad looked tired when he came home from work.

"Did you show that proposal to your boss?" asked Mom.

"We sure did," Dad said. "He turned us down without even looking at it."

"Well, he's done that before," Mom pointed out. "It's kind of a knee-jerk reaction when you show him a new idea. But after he thinks about it for a while, he usually listens."

MEANING: To react to something without thinking

Level playing field

"How were the dance team tryouts?" Lily asked her sister Erin.

"Better than I expected," Erin replied. "Ms. Ellis already knows some of the girls, and I was sure she had already made up her mind. But she was really nice to all of us, and she treated everybody the same. She said she'll let us know tomorrow."

"That's great!" said Lily. "You're really good, so I bet you'll make the team."

"All I wanted was a level playing field," Erin agreed. "I can do the rest."

MEANING: A fair chance; a chance to compete under fair conditions

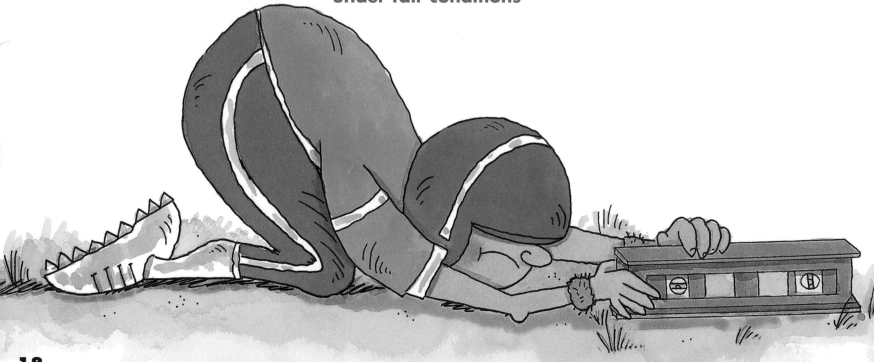

Mind your own beeswax

Allison was busy on the computer, making a card for her parents' anniversary. She wanted it to be a surprise to everybody, and she was almost done.

Just then her brother Alex came into the room. He wanted to use the computer, too. "What are you doing?" he asked, as she quickly covered the screen. "Come on, let me see!"

"Mind your own beeswax!" she said with a giggle. "It's a secret!"

MEANING: To mind your own business

Out like a light

The weekend of the soccer tournament was long and hot. Trevor had played in seven games. He didn't sleep well in the hotel. After the two-hour drive home, he went straight upstairs.

His dad went up to check on him later.

"How's he doing?" asked Mom when Dad came back downstairs.

Dad chuckled. "He's out like a light! He must have fallen asleep as soon as he went upstairs."

MEANING: To fall asleep right away

19

A penny for your thoughts

Melissa was happy. Her volleyball team had just won the championship! Best of all, she had played a great match! In her mind, she was picturing the game all over again. She was concentrating so hard, she didn't even hear her dad talking to her.

"Oh, sorry, Dad!" she said, shaking her head. "I didn't even hear you."

"A penny for your thoughts!" replied Dad. "Is everything okay?"

"Oh, yes!" answered Melissa. "I was just thinking about the game."

MEANING: To ask someone what they're thinking

Pull the plug

Jenna's family had planned to go to the waterpark, and they were supposed to leave soon. But Jenna was worried. Her six-year-old twin brothers kept arguing. They'd already gotten in trouble earlier, and each one kept blaming the other.

"Stop it, you guys!" Jenna said. "If you two don't behave, Mom and Dad are going to pull the plug on the whole trip!"

MEANING: To stop something; to say no to something

Raining cats and dogs

Miranda was sitting by the window, looking out at the gloomy weather.

"Phooey," she groaned. "This is terrible! We haven't been outside for three days. Is it ever going to stop raining?"

"Look at me!" exclaimed her brother, Jon, who had just finished his paper route. "I'm soaked. It's raining cats and dogs out there!"

MEANING: Raining hard; pouring rain

Saved by the bell

Jason and his brother were practicing jumps on their skateboards when Chase, an older neighbor, came by.

Chase said, "That jump's too small. Why don't you try the one at my house? I bet it's too much for you. I bet you're too scared."

"No, we're—" Jason started to reply. But just then he heard his dad calling them in for dinner.

"Whew, that was close!" Jason whispered as Chase walked away. "Saved by the bell!"

MEANING: To get out of something you don't want to do because something else comes up

Smell a rat

Aunt Maria had come to visit. "Mmmm," she said, sniffing. "Somebody's been baking cookies!"

"Not us!" said Gloria. "We don't have any cookies, do we?" She elbowed her little sister, who started giggling.

"No!" her sister squeaked, between giggles.

Aunt Maria put her hands on her hips. "I smell a rat!" she said. "You two are terrible liars. I think you've got some chocolate-chip cookies in here, and I'm going to find them!"

MEANING: To suspect something is wrong; to suspect that someone is not being honest or truthful

The third time's the charm

"Dad, can you believe it? We might be going to the state tournament!" exclaimed Anna. Her basketball team had just beaten a really tough team.

"Why are you so surprised? You've been playing well all year!" answered Dad.

"But Lincoln High beat us last year and the year before, too!" Anna said.

"Well," Dad replied with a smile, "you know what they say—the third time's the charm!"

MEANING: According to superstition, after two unsuccessful tries, the third time might be successful

The whole nine yards

Kelsey's big sister was graduating from high school in another month.

"She and her friends are really excited," Kelsey told her friend Emmy. "They can't stop talking about it."

"Are they going to do something to celebrate?" asked Emmy.

"They sure are!" Kelsey replied. "They're having a huge party—tons of food, decorations, music, lots of people—the whole nine yards."

MEANING: Everything